Copyright© 1977, Word Inc.
Copyright© 1999, 2017 by Gloria Jay Evans

The Wall
A Parable
by Gloria Jay Evans

Printed in the United States of America.

Library of Congress: 77-075460

ISBN 978-149-849-813-5

www.xulonpress.com

THE WALL

A PARABLE

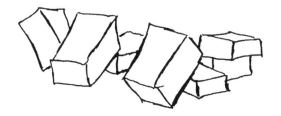

WRITTEN AND ILLUSTRATED BY
GLORIA JAY EVANS

TO MOTHER

I DON'T KNOW WHEN I FIRST
BEGAN TO BUILD THE WALL.

I SUPPOSE IT WAS WHEN IT
OCCURRED TO ME THAT I COULD
KEEP PEOPLE OUT OF MY LIFE
   BY BUILDING A SIMPLE WALL.
      THE WALL WOULD BE A
         KIND OF BOUNDARY—
         A
            KIND
               OF
               PROTECTION.

AT FIRST THE LITTLE WALL
WAS ONLY KNEE HIGH. IT
WAS REALLY QUITE
ATTRACTIVE, MADE OF
NATIVE STONE I
HAD FOUND IN MY
LIFE.

THE WALL WAS SO SMALL
THAT SOME PEOPLE DIDN'T
NOTICE IT___AND FELL FLAT
ON THEIR FACES.

OTHERS SAW IT BUT WOULD
STEP OVER IT AND COME
VERY CLOSE TO ME. I
FOUND THIS VERY
UNCOMFORTABLE. SO
I BUILT THE
WALL
HIGHER.

THIS WAS REALLY MUCH BETTER.
BUT SOON I FOUND THAT PEOPLE
WOULD COME AND REST THEIR
ARMS ON THE WALL WHILE TALKING
TO ME. SOME STAYED TOO LONG

AND SOME WERE NOT MY KIND
OF PEOPLE. AND EVEN WHEN I
EDGED THE TOP OF THE WALL
WITH SHARP STONES, THEY DIDN'T
SEEM TO NOTICE.

ONE DAY ONE OF THEM
   VAULTED OVER THE WALL
AND STOOD RIGHT INSIDE.
   THIS MADE ME ANGRY.
I DECIDED TO BUILD THE
   WALL HIGHER.

As I continued to build, I
became more and more self-
sufficient. I painted designs
on the stones. I made
arcs and colored windows
that distorted the light
so that one could neither
see in nor out.

THE WALL PLEASED ME SO THAT I
LONGED TO SHOW IT TO SOMEONE—
OR EXPLAIN HOW I HAD ACHIEVED
EACH DESIGN. BUT I REALIZED THAT
NO ONE HAD STOPPED BY TO TALK
FOR SOME TIME.

SOME WALKED BY NOT SEEMING
TO NOTICE ME OR MY WALL.
OTHERS STOOD SADLY BY
AND WATCHED ME BUILD. I
THOUGHT THEY WERE JEALOUS
OF MY WALL AND I RESENTED
THEM ___ ALL OF THEM.

HE WANTED TO COME INSIDE TO
 SEE WHAT I WAS DOING. I EXPLAINED
TO HIM THAT THE WHOLE PURPOSE
 OF THE WALL WAS TO KEEP
PEOPLE ON THE OTHER SIDE.
 BUT I COULD TELL HE DIDN'T
UNDERSTAND OR CARE. AS HE
 LEFT I WENT BACK TO BUILD
THE WALL HIGHER.

I BECAME SO ABSORBED IN MY WALL
THAT I FOUND LITTLE TIME FOR
ANYTHING ELSE. I SEARCHED MY
LIFE FOR NEW AND DIFFERENT
STONES. I FOUND STONES THAT
I DIDN'T EVEN KNOW I HAD.

THE DESIGN WAS VERY IMPORTANT
 TO ME. I WOULD BUILD AND
REBUILD UNTIL IT WAS JUST THE
 WAY I WANTED IT. SOME STONES
WERE SO DEAR TO ME THAT I
 POLISHED THEM CAREFULLY
SEVERAL TIMES A DAY.

THEN ONE DAY
I REALIZED THE
WALL WAS SO
HIGH THAT I NO
LONGER SAW
ANYONE GO BY.
I NO LONGER
HEARD
ANYONE.
EVERYTHING
WAS
QUIET.

—IS ANYONE THERE? I YELLED.

THERE WAS NO ANSWER. IT
WAS DARK INSIDE THE WALL
AND THE AIR WAS FOUL. I
SAT THERE FOR A LONG
TIME. IT WAS QUIET
AND DARK AND LONELY.

ONLY THE WHISPERS OF MY
MEMORIES COULD BE HEARD.

I THOUGHT OF THOSE WHO DID
NOT LIKE MY WALL, WHO HAD
LAUGHED AT IT, SCORNED IT,
BEEN JEALOUS OF IT. I SAT
IN THE SHADOWS AND LISTENED
FOR SOMEONE TO COME AND
TELL ME THAT THEY REALLY
LIKED IT. BUT IT WAS DARK
AND QUIET. VERY QUIET.

I DON'T KNOW HOW LONG I
SAT IN THE SHADOW OF MY
MEMORIES, BUT ONE DAY I
NOTICED THAT ONE OF THE
STONES DIDN'T MATCH
AS WELL AS I HAD THOUGHT
AND THE WALL
WAS CROOKED.
THIS WAS TOO
MUCH.

I HAD THOUGHT MY WALL WAS
PERFECT. BUT IT WAS NOT.
FRANTICALLY I EXAMINED THE WALL
AND SURE ENOUGH THERE WERE
OTHER
IMPERFECTIONS.

TO ADD TO THE PAIN OF MY
DISCOVERY, ONE DAY SOMEONE
YELLED FROM THE OTHER SIDE.

— YOUR WALL IS UGLY. IT IS
TWISTED AND GRAY AND
MISSHAPEN!

IT WAS THE DAY THE FLOWER
 FELL AT MY FEET THAT I BEGAN
TO CRY. I RAN TO THE WALL
 AND CLIMBED TO SEE WHO HAD
THROWN IT OVER.

BY THE
TIME I
REACHED
THE
TOP,

NO ONE
WAS THERE.

I RETURNED TO
THE FLOWER AND
SAT FOR A LONG
TIME LOOKING
AT ITS PERFECTION.

I BEGAN TO SEE
THE FOLLY
OF MY
WALL
AND
ITS
IMPERFECTION.

FLOODS OF TEARS BROUGHT ME
TO MY KNEES.

— OH, I AM SO ALONE. MY
WALL IS TOO HIGH. MY WALL
IS IMPERFECT AND UGLY.
EVERYTHING IS IN VAIN. I
HAVE NOTHING LEFT. WON'T
SOMEONE HELP ME __ PLEASE?

THEN A STRANGE THING HAPPENED.
SOMETHING INSIDE ME STIRRED AS
A BABY QUICKENS IN ITS
MOTHER'S WOMB. AND IN THE
STILLNESS OF MY BROKEN
WORLD I KNEW IN MY WHOLE
BEING A BLESSED PRESENCE. I
KNELT THERE IN WONDER
      THAT GOD WOULD
      COME TO ME.
      AND I WEPT
      WITH JOY THAT
      I WAS NOT
      ALONE ____

AND THAT MY DARKNESS
HAD BEEN PENETRATED
      BY HIS BLESSED LIGHT.

FOR DAYS I STOOD IN THE
JOY OF HIS PRESENCE. MY WALL
SHONE WITH THE WARMTH OF
HIS LIGHT AND I NO LONGER
FELT COLD AND ALONE. I
KNEW THAT HE HAD WATCHED
ME BUILD MY WALL AND
THAT HE HAD WAITED PATIENTLY
FOR ME TO SEE IT WAS
IN VAIN.

FINALLY IT OCCURRED TO ME THAT
HE WOULD KNOW WHY MY WALL
WAS SO UGLY. WHEN I ASKED HIM,
HE BEGAN TO TEACH ME. DAY BY
DAY HE SHOWED ME MY ERROR.
HE GAVE THE STONES NAMES.

— THIS STONE IS JEALOUSY.
YOU MUST REMOVE IT.

SOMETIMES I WOULD BE RE-
LUCTANT. FOR DAYS I WOULD
PROTEST. THIS WAS MY FAVORITE
STONE. IT WAS ONE I HAD
SAVED AND CHERISHED FOR YEARS.

WHEN I WAS FINALLY READY,
HE HELPED ME REMOVE
THE STONE.

ONE DAY
WHEN WE HAD
REMOVED ONE OF
THE HEAVIER STONES,
A HAND CAME THROUGH
THE OPENING.

— TAKE IT, HE SAID.

HESITANTLY I TOOK THE
HAND. FOR A LONG TIME
I STOOD IN THE WARMTH
OF THAT GRASP. SOMEHOW
I KNEW THE HAND AND
THE ONE BEHIND IT HAD
BEEN WAITING FOR AN
OPENING IN MY WALL.

THERE STIRRED IN ME A HUNGER
AND A LONGING FOR HUMAN
COMFORT.

AT FIRST I THOUGHT HIS PRESENCE
WITHIN MY WALL WAS ENOUGH. BUT
WITH THE COMING OF THE HAND CLASP,
I KNEW HE HAD COME TO TEAR THE
WALL DOWN. A PART OF ME WANTED
TO SPRING FORTH BUT ANOTHER PART
OF ME CRIED
OUT IN FEAR.
WHY COULDN'T
I KEEP A PART
OF THE WALL?
HIS PRESENCE
WAS
ENOUGH.

I LOOKED AT ALL THE STONES I
HAD COLLECTED THROUGHOUT MY LIFE.
SOME WERE STILL IN THE WALL.
THE OTHERS HE HAD STACKED NEATLY
IN A CORNER. IF I EVER CHOSE
TO REBUILD THE WALL, I COULD. I
BEGGED HIM TO THROW THEM AWAY
BUT HE TOLD ME THAT IN THEM I
COULD TEST MY STRENGTH.

HOW THEY TEMPTED ME!

ONE DAY WHEN HE DIDN'T SEEM
TO BE AROUND, I DASHED OVER
AND PICKED UP A CHERISHED STONE
TO REBUILD MY WALL. IT WAS
THEN I REALIZED THAT IF I WERE
TO BE STRONG ENOUGH TO LIVE
WITHOUT THE WALL, I WOULD
HAVE TO KNOW THE STONES
WERE THERE. I WOULD HAVE TO
KNOW THE NAME OF EACH ONE.
IN KNOWING THEIR NAMES,
    I COULD NOT
     USE THEM AGAIN
      WITHOUT BETRAYING
       HIM.

AS WE REMOVED MORE STONES, THE
LIGHT CAME IN. AND HIS LIGHT
WOULD SHINE OUT. I BEGAN TO
LOOK THROUGH THE OPEN PLACES.

I COULD SEE THINGS I HADN'T
NOTICED FOR A LONG TIME —
DEWDROPS, LADYBUGS, SUN BEAMS,
AND BLADES OF GRASS.

HE TOLD ME MANY THINGS AND
GAVE ME GIFTS. THE MORE I
TALKED TO HIM THE MORE I
WANTED TO TALK TO HIM.
I SAW THINGS I HAD
NEVER SEEN BEFORE
AND HEARD THINGS I
HAD NEVER HEARD
BEFORE.

ONE DAY AS I WAS STANDING BY
  AN OPEN PLACE, A MAN STOPPED
TO TALK. I TOLD HIM ABOUT THE
BLESSED PRESENCE AND HOW HE
HAD CHANGED MY LIFE. THE MAN
SAID HE UNDERSTOOD.

   — BUT, HE SAID, IF THAT'S
   TRUE, WHY DO YOU HAVE
   THIS BLOCK OF RESENTMENT
   IN YOUR WALL? I CAN'T
   SEE HIM. THE STONE
   BLOCKS THE WAY.

I LOOKED AND SURE ENOUGH, ONE OF
MY MOST PRIZED ROCKS LAY DIRECTLY
IN FRONT OF ME COVERING NEARLY
ONE SIDE OF THE WALL.

IT HAD BEEN ONE OF THE
FIRST STONES I HAD PLACED.
IT WAS A LARGE CONGLOMERATE
OF DISILLUSIONMENT, CHILDISHNESS,
STUBBORNNESS, AND OTHER PETTY
STONES.

I ASKED THE MAN IF HE WOULD
HELP ME REMOVE IT. I WAS SO ASHAMED
THE BLESSED PRESENCE MIGHT SEE
THIS LARGE ROCK.

THE MAN DID LOOSEN THE
STONE AND I THANKED HIM
AS HE WENT ON HIS WAY.

I WONDERED HOW I COULD EVER
REMOVE THAT STONE WITHOUT
HELP.

I REALLY TRIED. I TUGGED AND TUGGED AND STRUGGLED AND STRUGGLED BUT IT ONLY MOVED SLIGHTLY. I SAT DOWN IN DESPAIR. I KNEW THE MAN WAS RIGHT. THE STONE MUST BE REMOVED.

— OH DEAR, I SAID. HOW CAN I EVER REMOVE THIS ONE! IT IS SO BIG AND I AM SO WEAK.

— YOU CANNOT MOVE IT, HE SAID.

— BUT I MUST, I REPLIED. THE MAN SAID HE COULD HARDLY BELIEVE YOU WERE HERE WITH THAT STONE IN THE WALL.

— IF YOU REALLY WANT THE STONE REMOVED, I WILL REMOVE IT.

WE WENT CAREFULLY OVER TO THE WALL AND CHIPPED AWAY EACH SMALL STONE UNTIL THE LARGE ONE WAS DIMINISHED.

EVEN WITH THE STONE OF RESENTMENT
GONE, PEOPLE KEPT STUMBLING OVER
DEBRIS AND REMNANTS OF THE WALL
AS THEY WALKED THROUGH MY LIFE.

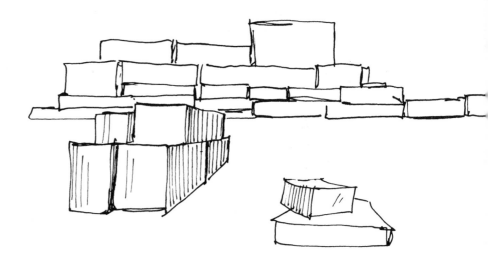

THERE WAS A WOMAN WHO KNEW HIM
AND HAD LET HIM TEAR DOWN HER WALL.
SHE WALKED IN AND SAT DOWN ON ONE
OF THE STONES. I TOLD HER WHAT HE
HAD DONE FOR ME AND SHE TOLD ME
WHAT HE HAD DONE FOR HER.

I TOLD HER HOW I HAD SUFFERED SO
AND THAT I WOULD NEVER FORGET HOW
FORSAKEN AND LONELY I HAD FELT
INSIDE MY WALL.

— YES, SHE SAID, SELF-PITY IS
A TERRIBLE THING.

WHEN SHE LEFT I FOUND THE STONE
OF SELF-PITY IN MY WALL. IT WAS
WET WITH MY TEARS. I DRIED IT OFF
AND LAID IT WITH THE OTHER STONES.

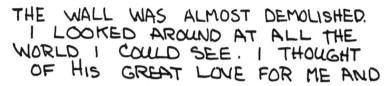

THE WALL WAS ALMOST DEMOLISHED.
I LOOKED AROUND AT ALL THE
WORLD I COULD SEE. I THOUGHT
OF HIS GREAT LOVE FOR ME AND
BREATHED A
DEEP SIGH OF
SATISFACTION AND
PRIDE THAT I
SHOULD HAVE
COME SO FAR.

— LOOK HOW MUCH I HAVE
ACCOMPLISHED, I THOUGHT. HOW
MUCH BETTER I KNOW HIM THAN
SOME OF THOSE OTHERS OUT
THERE. POOR UNENLIGHTENED
ONES WHO DON'T KNOW HIM
NEARLY AS WELL AS I. IT IS
SO EASY. WHY CAN'T THEY SEE?

OVERWHELMED BY ALL HE HAD DONE
FOR ME AND ALL HE HAD TAUGHT ME,
I STOOD UPON ONE OF THE REMAINING
STONES AND BEGAN TO TELL ANYONE
WHO PASSED BY WHAT THE BLESSED
PRESENCE HAD DONE FOR ME.

I WAS APPALLED THAT NO ONE SEEMED
TO HEAR OR UNDERSTAND WHAT I
WAS SAYING. I TOLD THEM HOW DARK
AND LONELY IT HAD BEEN INSIDE THE
WALL. AND HOW HE HAD COME TO
HELP ME TEAR IT DOWN. HOW
VAIN IT WAS TO BUILD WALLS.

I NOTICED OTHERS WORKING ON WALLS
AND RAN OVER TO PLEAD WITH
THEM TO STOP, BUT NO ONE
WOULD LISTEN.

IN MY FRUSTRATION I CRIED OUT

– WHY CAN'T THEY HEAR?
  WHY CAN'T THEY UNDERSTAND?
  WHY CAN'T THEY BELIEVE ME?

I LAY FACE DOWN ON THE
STONE I HAD STOOD UPON.
IT WAS EXTREMELY LARGE,
HIGHLY POLISHED. IT HAD
BEEN MY GREAT PRIZE. IT
WAS MORE THAN LIFE SIZE.

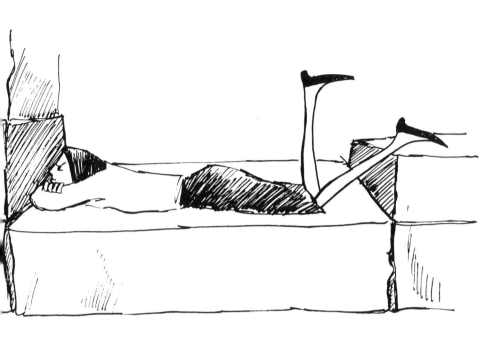

— DO YOU WANT THE ANSWER
TO YOUR QUESTIONS? HE ASKED.

— YOU KNOW I DO, I SIGHED.

— RAISE YOUR HEAD AND LOOK
AT THE STONE YOU ARE
LYING UPON.

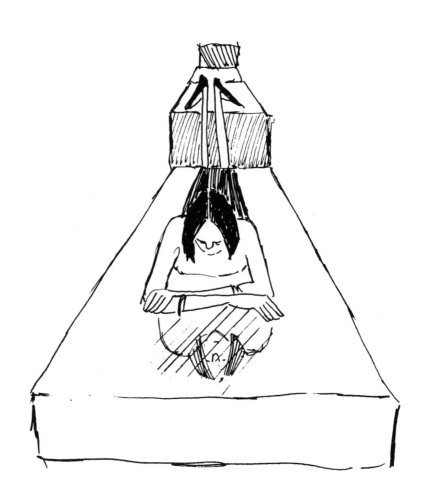

I RAISED MY HEAD AND GASPED
FOR I SAW MY OWN REFLECTION
IN THE MASSIVE STONE. THERE
WAS PRIDE IN MY LOOK AND
MANNER. I KNEW THE STONE
WAS PRIDE. QUIETLY WE
REMOVED IT.

NOW WE COULD SEE BEYOND THE
MEADOW AND A PATH LED FORTH
FROM WHERE I STOOD. THEN
HE SAID A STRANGE THING

— NOW YOU MUST GO. I
WILL GO WITH YOU AND
YET I WILL STAY HERE.

— BUT I DON'T WANT TO
LEAVE, I PROTESTED. THE
WALL STILL STANDS. THERE
ARE OTHER STONES TO
REMOVE. I WANT TO BE
HERE WITH YOU.

— I SAID I WOULD GO WITH YOU.
THERE IS AN OPENING IN THE
WALL FOR YOU TO COME AND GO.
DO YOU REMEMBER THE FLOWER
THAT FELL AT YOUR FEET, THE
HAND THAT YOU CLASPED, THE
WOMAN WHO SHOWED YOU SELF-PITY
OR THE MAN WHO SHOWED YOU
RESENTMENT?

— OH YES, I SIGHED, OH YES.

— THEN YOU MUST GO AND DO
LIKEWISE. FOR TO WHOM MUCH
IS GIVEN, MUCH IS EXPECTED.
WHEREVER YOU GO I GO WITH
YOU. AND WHENEVER YOU
COME BACK HERE TO BE
TEMPTED OR TO REMOVE
MORE STONES I WILL BE
HERE.

SO I WENT FORTH. SOON I SAW A
  WALL BUILDER. HE HAD JUST
STARTED TO BUILD HIS WALL. I
  SAW PAIN AND HURT IN HIS
FACE — AND CONFUSION IN HIS FRENZY
  TO BUILD. I LEANED AGAINST THE
WALL WANTING TO TELL HIM I
  UNDERSTOOD. BUT THE STONES WERE
PLACED SO THAT THE SHARP EDGES
  CUT ME AND I RETREATED IN
PAIN.

  I STOOD BY THE WALL
  NURSING MY WOUNDS. IN
  SADNESS I WATCHED
  HIM BUILD.

SOON HIS WALL WAS SO HIGH I
COULD NOT SEE HIM AND MY
HEART ACHED BECAUSE I KNEW
IT WAS DARK AND LONELY INSIDE.
I CALLED TO HIM BUT HE COULD
NOT HEAR. THE UGLINESS OF
THE WALL WAS UNBELIEVABLE. I
REACHED OUT AND TOUCHED IT,
LEANED AGAINST IT.

I DON'T KNOW HOW LONG I WAS
THERE BUT ONE DAY I HEARD
SOMEONE YELL,

      — YOUR WALL IS UGLY. IT
         IS TWISTED AND GRAY
         AND MISSHAPEN.

STRANGELY, THOUGH I HAD NEVER
HEARD A SOUND FROM THE
WALL BEFORE, GREAT RACKING
SOBS EXPLODED FROM INSIDE.
TEARS STREAMED DOWN MY
FACE AND I CRIED OUT IN
FRUSTRATION,

     — WON'T YOU HELP HIM
       PLEASE? PLEASE?

I THOUGHT MY HEART WOULD
BREAK. IN DESPERATION I
LOOKED ABOUT. IF ONLY I
COULD GIVE HIM A GIFT TO
EASE HIS PAIN.

I LOOKED DOWN TO FIND A
SMALL FLOWER AT MY FEET.
HASTILY I PLUCKED IT AND
THREW IT OVER THE WALL.

THEN THE SOBBING STOPPED
 AND I KNEW A GREAT PEACE FOR
IN SOME STRANGE WAY I KNEW
 THAT THE BLESSED PRESENCE HAD
COME TO HIM AND THAT MY ACHING
 HEART AND THE GIFT OF THE
FLOWER HAD HELPED BRING IT
 ABOUT.

I KNEW THAT SOON THERE WOULD
 BE AN OPENING IN THE WALL,
AND I COULD GRASP HIS HAND. I
 KNEW, TOO, THAT HE MIGHT NEVER
KNOW THAT IT WAS I WHO WAS
 THERE. BUT IT REALLY DIDN'T MATTER
FOR IN SOME WONDERFUL WAY, I
 HAD BECOME A PART OF EVERY MAN'S
LIFE. THROUGH THE BLESSED PRESENCE
 WE WOULD ALL BECOME ONE.
SOMEHOW I KNEW I WOULD NEVER
 BE THE SAME.

I RETURNED TO MY WALL AND
THE BLESSED PRESENCE WAS THERE.
TOGETHER WE REMOVED THE
STONES OF FEAR,
MISTRUST,
AND INDIFFERENCE.

— HE SAID,
NOW YOU BEGIN TO UNDERSTAND
LOVE. WITHOUT LOVE ALL THE THINGS
I HAVE TOLD YOU WOULD BE
MEANINGLESS. YOU WILL BEGIN
TO LIVE IN PEACE AND UNDER-
STANDING. YOU WILL LEARN
GENTLENESS AND KINDNESS. BUT
IT WILL TAKE TIME. I WILL
ALWAYS BE IN YOU.

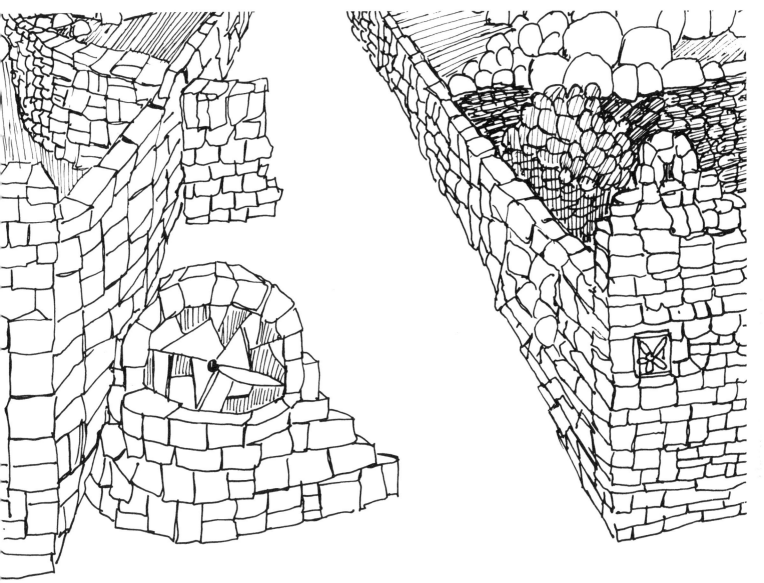

SOMETIMES JUST WAITING BESIDE A WALL,
SOMETIMES TOSSING A FLOWER,
SOMETIMES GRASPING A HAND.

THERE ARE DAYS THAT I RETURN
TO MY WALL. I TOUCH THE
STACKED STONES AND
EXAMINE THE
REMNANTS OF
MY WALL.

AT TIMES I AM FILLED WITH
A DESIRE TO REBUILD IT, BUT
WE TALK AND HE HELPS ME
TO BE STRONG. SOMETIMES
WE
REMOVE
ANOTHER
STONE.

IT IS STRANGE THAT I BEGIN TO
RECOGNIZE OTHERS LIKE MYSELF.
WHEN I SEE SOMEONE WITH A
FLOWER, I KNOW THAT IT WILL
BE THROWN OVER A WALL. SOME-
TIMES I SEE SOMEONE STANDING
BY A WALL SADLY WATCHING A
WALL BUILDER. I SEE THOSE
WHO ARE SITTING ON STONES
EXPLAINING WHAT KIND OF STONES
THEY HAVE USED.

I KNOW THE BLESSED PRESENCE IS
  WITH THEM, TOO. WE PASS ON THE
PATH AND A GREAT LOVE PASSES
  BETWEEN US. I SEE PEACE IN
THEIR EYES AND FAITH IN THEIR
  HEARTS AND I KNOW THAT
SOMEDAY THE WALLS WILL BE
DOWN AND WE WILL ALL
WALK FREE FROM PLACE TO
  PLACE ___

        THE
        GREAT
        FAMILY
        OF
        GOD.

EVANS ENTERPRISES • 701 East 38th Street • Sioux Falls, SD 57105

CPSIA information can be obtained
at www.ICGtesting.com
Printed in the USA
LVHW10s0350021018
592105LV00024B/2016/P